ANECDOTES
OF A PASTOR'S WIFE

May God bless your ministry.

Elaine

Anecdotes of a Pastor's Wife

Elaine Smith

Copyright © 2019 by Elaine Smith

All rights reserved. This book or any portion thereof may not be reproduced or transmitted in any form or manner, electronic or mechanical, including photocopying, recording, or by any information storage or retrieval system, without the express written permission of the copyright owner except for the use of brief quotations in a book review or other noncommercial uses permitted by copyright law.

Printed in the United States of America

Library of Congress Control Number: 2019910091
ISBN: Softcover   978-1-64376-274-6
         eBook   978-1-64376-275-3

Republished by: PageTurner, Press and Media LLC
Publication Date: 07/23/2019

To order copies of this book, contact:
PageTurner, Press and Media
Phone: 1-888-447-9651
order@pageturner.us
www.pageturner.us

PAGETURNER
PRESS AND MEDIA

Contents

Acknowledgments vii

Chapter 1: The Beginning 1

Chapter 2: Some of My Most Memorable People 14

Chapter 3: Home Life 36

Chapter 4: Me—A Secretary? 53

Chapter 5: Chaplaincy Service 58

Chapter 6: Amazing Testimonies from Overseas 77

Conclusion 97

Acknowledgments

I would like to thank my dear husband for making this wonderful life possible. He put up with me through it all for which I am grateful.

I also wish to thank my dear friends and many pastors' wives who encouraged me to get this book finished.

Also, thank you to Shirley Jewell and Cindy Janota, who helped me with the editing, ideas, and getting it finished. It is appreciated.

The Bible quotations used are from the King James Version.

Chapter 1

The Beginning

When I was a little girl, my mother always said, "You will be a farmer's wife or else a preacher's wife someday." I didn't really understand her prophetic words, but I do remember loving animals and going to church. I still do.

I remember that going to church was a happy time. Everybody there was friendly to me, and it was peaceful. I loved the screeching of the old ladies as they tried to sing; I would giggle at them. I loved the piano player chewing her gum as she made the old piano come alive in the little country church.

Well, my mom was right on one part. I did become a pastor's wife. She also said that if I were a pastor's wife, I would be as poor as a pauper. On that point, Mom was wrong. I have been a wealthy woman enjoying fully the blessings of God daily in my life.

As a child, I had a home with two parents, four sisters, and a twin brother. We considered ourselves "Christians" as the entire family attended church without fail on Christmas, Easter, and other occasions throughout the year.

Our home life was not without its challenges. I lived in lots of fear as my house was haunted. There were places in our house where no one wanted to be. The spirit of a little man lived in the attic. He would lift the attic door on full moon time, and it would be open for two or three days. The full moon was terrible. I slept with a pillow over my head every night to muffle the sounds coming from the attic. I think the little man was singing. It was in a monotone, and if I shouted "Quit that noise" in anger, he would change to another note. I have many memories of our haunted house. My sister and I saw him walking across our bedroom to the stairs one day, and we threw our slippers at him. They went right through him and hit the wall. I always felt sorry for my sisters that had to sleep in the room with the attic door.

Our town had lots of witches in it, and they were active. It was a small town, and most of the people in that town were oppressed by the occultist influence. Witches lived on both sides of our property, and we never wanted to go outside at night as it was scary.

As scary as that may have been, as a teen, Mom told me to take a babysitting job. I was to babysit two little boys. That sounds okay, but the family owned and lived in a funeral home. By law, they were not allowed to leave a corpse unattended, so if the family went away and a corpse was in the building, guess who was the sitter?

When the children were left at home in my care, they were in bed already. Their beds were on the top floor of the house. My assigned duty for the night was to be in the family room in the basement. The basement also had a room for fresh bodies waiting for embalming. I knew that, and it was pretty creepy having to stay there until the bars closed and the owners returned home. While waiting for them to come home, the only thing I could do was watch television. It was way too creepy to stay in a silent house with no TV or source of noise. The big problem was that there was only one thing airing on television that late at night . . . *Dracula* movies. That dramatically added to my anxiety and fears. When the family came home, it was usually about one in the morning. They would pay me, and I would run home. It was always dark, and I ran from tree to tree, stopping to look before I went further. Then I went into my haunted house and up to my bedroom. I always prayed the "Now I Lay Me Down to Sleep" as I quickly crawled into bed.

On occasion, my twin brother and I would sneak over to the neighbor's house and watch a séance through her window. Halloween was a particularly fearful night as someone in our community would usually die a tragic death.

I became a true Christian on my senior year of high school. I was at church camp where I was told that Jesus loves me, and he had a plan for my life. Also I learned that if I followed his plan, I would be blessed. As far as I knew, I had never met a Christian, at least one my age. I didn't know anything about being a Christian. I knew I wanted the peace, forgiveness, and security God offered. The Lord Jesus forgave me and my sin that day, and I have never been the same. My fear was gone. My comfort was in the Lord. I read the Bible every day after that and prayed. The oppression of the demonic spirits in my house no longer plagued me. As I left camp that week, I asked God to show me some Christians that would help me to live the Christian life.

God began answering my prayers right after I got home from camp. The day after I arrived home, I walked downtown to the post office to get the mail. I was surprised that there were people living at the former vacant house across the street. I saw girls around my age standing in front. I went over to introduce myself to them. I asked them their names. "Pat and Peggy Friend," they answered. "Friend is your last name?" I inquired. "Yes," they replied. "I suppose you are Christians?" I asked as I secretly thought of my prayer.

"Yes, we are Christians" was their immediate response.

We became instant friends as I shared my new faith with them.

After I arrived home from my camp experience, I found myself more serious about the future. I decided to go to college after high school. After I finished high school at Yale, my parents divorced. I moved to the city to live with my dad. There I could walk to junior college classes. I spent some time in the student lounge with a group of Christian fellowship students daily. They would ask me pertinent questions about my salvation. Convinced that I was a believer, they then quizzed me on my baptism. I told them I was sprinkled as a young child in church on a Sunday. They told me to look in the Bible where I would discover that if I wasn't saved before baptism, then I wasn't baptized. I only got a wet head. They also told me that Jesus gave the example of baptism for all of us. The Gospels all talk about being saved and then being baptized. In the Bible, baptism is always going into the water, under the water, and back out of the water. I read it time and again in the scriptures, studying over and over, and decided I needed to be scripturally baptized.

I did get baptized in the water at the local church. It was live on the radio, and I had to give a public testimony over the airwaves. God helped me through that. I decided then and there that I needed to study the Bible more, so I could understand the Bible myself instead of trusting someone to spoon-feed me. I decided to attend a Bible college the next year.

I applied at Pillsbury Baptist Bible College in Owatonna, Minnesota, and was accepted. I loved it. While in Bible college, I took a wonderful class called "The Pastor's Wife." It was a great class led by Mrs. Thelma Cedarholm. It was so practical. I have used it and thought about it every year since. I will always be grateful for my mentor, Mrs. Cedarholm. She was great!

My fiancé, Dave, was a little perplexed or even disturbed when I took that class. "Who are you going to marry?" he asked me. "I am not going to be a pastor," he emphatically stated. I just answered, "It never hurts to learn all I can about everything."

Dave did become a pastor, and I have now been a pastor's wife for over forty-five years. I consider it a wonderful calling from the Lord for both of us. It is a tremendous privilege to be able to serve the Lord in this way. It has provided joy, plenty of sorrow, plenty of humor, trials, and tons of blessings.

I have three sons and three daughters-in-law that love my Lord and eight grandchildren growing in their love for the Lord Jesus Christ. God is good to me.

I have had the privilege of meeting believers in Ireland, Scotland, England, Ukraine, Russia, Mexico, and the United States. I have been in Turkey for four times to meet, teach, and witness to new believers. It is nothing short of a blessed life lived for God who gives us abundantly above all that we could ever ask or think.

That said, I would like to say that I believe having been a pastor's wife for over forty-five years has been great. It has been full of laughter, sorrow, tears, fun, guests, cooking, counseling, teaching, loving, and being loved by many people in all walks of life. What a privilege and honor to be trusted by others in confidence and be able to help them along in their Christian walk. I have made many cherished friendships for life and am grateful for each one.

Pastor and I determined from the beginning that we would team up for counseling. We have both been trained, and in the case of a woman needing help, I would always be there, especially in marriage counseling. It is wiser and safer for everyone involved. It really puts a woman at ease to know she is also represented by a woman who understands her situation. God has blessed our feeble efforts and used us to repair many marriages, relationships, and broken lives. It is always a thrill and a blessing to see a happy ending.

It was interesting in different churches and communities to see how people think about things. In one community, a lady wanted my husband to perform her daughter's wedding in our church. He asked her where they had attended church. Her comment was, "Oh, our church is through the television. We listen to Reverend So-and-So every week. He is our pastor."

My husband, who is never excited about performing a wedding for strangers, answered the lady with, "I think Pastor So-and-So should do the wedding. He is your pastor." "Oh," she reported, "he is much too busy and far away in another state to do this wedding." My husband responded, "Well, maybe you should consider a local church. I am not interested in doing work for a television evangelist whom I've never met. Surely, he knows your daughter better than I do. A pastor knows his flock, and I don't know your daughter. If you choose to come to our local church, it could be possible in the future, but no, I will not marry a stranger. A wedding is sacred before God, not to be taken lightly." She left to find someone else. We never saw her again.

At another church where we served, pastor was doing a special service—the reason I just don't recall. After the service, pastor and I stood at the door to shake hands with everyone. A nice-looking lady came by with some friends in the line. She introduced her friends saying, "This is my pastor, Pastor Smith." We had never seen her before and did not know her name. That is when we discovered that the whole little community considered our church and this pastor to be their very own. If they ever wanted to attend or needed a pastor, this was the one. We were the only church for ten miles. We belonged to them because we lived there. We learned to love them all.

One time, while visiting a lady who attended church that previous Sunday, we were approached with a rather unusual question: "Can your church let me be a member and teach Sunday school if I work in a bar as a dancer? I am not on welfare and make a living for my son, and I honestly earn my own way."

We welcomed her to come to church but also explained God's standard for a believer's life. God says, "Be ye holy as I am holy." That bar was far from holy, and topless dancing didn't fit the picture, either. Perhaps there was other employment she could pursue. She displayed knowledge of the Bible, but it was for her private interpretation. We never saw her again.

In trying to be all things to all people and reaching out, I was challenged to take up golfing. Ha! We won't dwell on that skill I never perfected, but it proved to be an effective choice. A lady in the church told me about her mother. She said her mother needed a new friend, and if I could befriend her, she would probably come to church. I bought clubs and golfed with her. Well, the lady was right; her mother and I became instant friends, and she has been faithfully coming to church ever since and is a sweet believer.

On another occasion, pastor and I called upon a couple who were artists. They both taught art and loved art. They came to church for which we rejoiced. Then they asked us to please join their "Adults Learn to Paint" class. "What a joke! Me, learn to paint?" I responded. They persisted, and we joined the class. It was more fun than I figured it would be. Trying new things is an art! Pastor and I each have a large picture hanging in our workrooms today—masterpieces we joyfully painted in their class.

Although my life verse has to do with "do all things without murmuring and complaint," I had to be reminded a while back by the dear Lord not to complain. We had lived in the country where evening noises were whip-poor-wills, coyotes, owls, and wildlife. The daytime noises were from dozens of species of birds. I loved trying to identify each sound and to find the bird making it. One time, I heard a bird fly over and repeat "Timmy, come play" a number of times. It was a catbird mocking the neighbor boys as they called our son over to their house. I loved it. What a place to live.

We left the country and moved to our city home. Of course, all the noises were different: trains, ambulances, police cars, etc. However, the birds were all sparrows. We had no trees on the land, and sparrows were everywhere singing beautifully—but only sparrows.

One day in a grumbling attitude, I told the Lord I would like another kind of bird to add to the sparrows. I am sick of just sparrows. God heard my prayer and answered appropriately. The next morning, I saw one of the most beautiful birds I have ever seen. It was very colorful, and it sang a nice different song than the sparrow. I immediately thanked the dear Lord for that bird as I passed it on my way outside going to work. I was so thrilled! How great our God is to answer such a trite prayer so quickly.

After a couple of days, I started noticing dead sparrows on the lawn. I wondered why. I looked in my bird book to try to identify the new bird. Well, guess what? It was a northern shrike, known for killing smaller birds. Soon, I had no sparrows left. No birds of any kind would fill my yard now.

I asked the Lord to forgive me as the shrike moved to better hunting grounds. All my sparrows were gone, and the shrike left as well.

I complained, and it was wrong. I asked God to help me be more grateful and to please give me back some sparrows. He is a gracious God, and that spring, more sparrows moved in. I thanked God for them and enjoyed their music with gratefulness. God is so good. I love sparrows more than ever now. I know God sees every sparrow that falls to the ground. What a great God we have!

At one church, we were blessed to have three beautiful piano players. Two of them were concert pianists and very gifted. After enjoying them in church for a couple of years, I found out that they all were going to move away the same fall. I was devastated. I began praying for a new pianist to come to our church. We had just three months before they all were to leave, and I didn't know any pianist who could play the piano for our church. One day, three different people told me that I should learn to play the piano. One lady offered to teach me for the three months she had left before she moved. Praying to God for help and wisdom, I decided to try to learn the piano from this lady before she left. It seemed God was leading me that direction.

I did not own a piano. The church was nineteen steps from my back door to its back door. I had one lesson a week and practiced about sixty hours between lessons. God helped me, and when the family moved, I was ready to take pianist duties. I'm certainly not a concert pianist, but I can play most hymns at tempo for the congregation. I was scared but knew God wanted me to do that, so I did. He has blessed me. Thank you, Lord, again for your mercy!

On the first Sunday that I played for the church service, my husband, Pastor Smith, told the congregation that he had a checklist for being the perfect pastor's wife. I had met them all in his eyes except for being a piano player. He signaled over to me at the piano and said, "Now I have a perfect wife." What a lovely tribute from a wonderful husband! I have played for over twelve years now at church.

I cannot suggest that you necessarily follow my paths, for the stories found in this book are unique to me. Some were the results of bad judgment on my part and some from just plain inexperience. Yet others were wonderful experiences. All were of God's grace to me. Everybody has a story to tell, and I have decided to write mine in a book. It is my goal to entertain you, bless you, and to hopefully challenge you to enjoy serving a wonderful God as much as I do.

As a hostess, I had some interesting experiences. Once, a missionary man visited, stayed for lunch, telling me nothing about his special dietary health needs. I served BBQ sandwiches, chips, pickles, and carrot and celery sticks. After the prayer for our meal, Richard, the missionary, took the meat bowl and emptied it all onto his plate. He left us the hamburger buns with nothing to put on them. He smiled, took a big bite, and said, "I don't like veggies, and I don't eat bread." In all fairness, most of the hundreds of missionaries staying with us over the years were jewels, helping us wherever they could. Many of them entertained our boys beautify and were a great blessing to us all.

Pastor always worked hard at secular jobs while ministering in small churches. He often took the night shift. The boys would climb up on our bed and drive cars all over him while he was sleeping in the daytime. When I asked what they were doing, they simply replied in childlike faith, "Playing with Daddy."

Yes, Dave was a sound sleeper. I used that to my advantage one year as I needed to paint our bedroom. I could not paint while the children were awake, so I painted when everyone else was asleep, including my husband. I moved the bed, did the ceiling and all four walls that night. When he awoke, he looked a little perplexed. Something was different. Then it hit him: the walls were a different color. He jumped out of bed to see if his hair was painted. He had no clue that I did it during the night. Such fun I had!

Chapter 2

Some of My Most Memorable People

All of the names in this book have been changed, but the stories are all true.

Edna

I must tell you about sweet little Edna. She was a logger, former logger's wife, Sunday school teacher, and a dear friend. Little Edna even babysat for us a couple of times, and the children loved her. In time, dear Edna had a stroke and moved away from our town to live with her family. We lost contact with her a couple of years ago. Pastor and I, along with our three boys, have a nursing home service in two nursing homes in town each Sunday. One Sunday afternoon, I noticed little Edna's name on the roster. I asked the nurses to please go get Edna. I mentioned that she was my friend, and I wanted her in our service. "Oh, you don't want her. She's a vegetable. She doesn't know anybody and can't talk," the nurse advised us.

"I don't care. She's my friend, and I want her here. Please go get her," I responded. Reluctantly, they went to get her. They brought her out in her wheelchair with her head resting on a tray. I spoke to her, but she didn't know me.

At about that time, the pastor started the worship service. We started to sing a hymn. Sweet little Edna sat up in her chair and loudly sang every word of every verse. The nurses were amazed and ran to get all the other nurses to watch Edna sing. We sang two more hymns, and again, she sang along with us sitting up straight and smiling.

At the end of our service, we talked to little Edna. She knew who we were—pastor and wife of the church. She did not know which pastor and wife. The nurses all came over to hear her talk. I decided to show those nurses how a vegetable can give the Gospel salvation plan. I asked little Edna to quote Romans 3:23. She did it perfectly. Then she quoted Romans 10:9–10, Romans 6:23, and John 3:16. She quoted them all accurately, giving the complete plan of salvation to six nurses who did not believe she could even talk. They were amazed.

God is so good. If there is life, where the Spirit of God is, God can always minister. God never leaves his own people and he never will. Edna did not talk again all week, but the next week when we arrived, she sang with us again. She did that every week until the Lord took her home. Each week, nurses came to watch her sing and were amazed how this little vegetable could worship the Lord. God honored her and blessed us with her. We will never forget that experience!

Granny

God also blessed us with a little granny. Granny was a farmer's wife. She had a lot of skills that most of us know nothing about. My mother-in-law and I went to visit Granny one morning and found her in the kitchen bent over a big bucket. I walked over to look in the bucket and saw two pig heads. "What are you doing?" I asked.

She was making head cheese. The heads were all boiled until tender, and she was scraping all the meat off the skulls. She would then pack the meat into loaf pans and chill it. After that, it was ready to be sliced and eaten. At that moment, I went outside to hoe the garden. I let Mom and Granny eat the head cheese.

Granny's Friend

Granny had a very good friend in the nursing home. She had witnessed to her for about fifty years. She asked me to go show her how to be a Christian. I was very happy to do that. I visited the lady and found her to be very receptive and wanting to be a Christian. I taught her how she could pray the sinner's prayer asking Jesus to save her. She did that in her Swedish accent. She looked up at me with a beautiful smile and said, "Dat is the first time I ever did pray." I gave her a couple of more scripture verses and asked her if she had a Bible. "Vall," she said, "Vee learned to read from the Bible as a child. Of course, I have a Bible. Do you think I am stupid? Dat vas the only book vee ever owned." This dear lady was eighty-five years old. She learned to read from the Bible as a child. God said, "My Word shall not return void." It took many years for her, but the power of the Word of God bore fruit. She changed and gave good testimony of her new faith to all around her. She lived about a year after that time. Granny was so happy when her friend told her of her new trust in Jesus as her Savior. Thank you, Lord, for that opportunity!

Annie Fay

I wasn't married very long when Annie Fay asked me for help. As a young pastor's wife, I said, "Sure, I'll come over to your house this week sometime."

Annie Fay was a good twenty years older than me. She met me at the door and expressed that she had a problem getting her husband to notice her or pay her any attention at all. She said, "Honey, you and your husband seem so in love. Can you help me? My husband comes home, grabs dinner, and sits in front of the TV. He hardly says 'hi' even. What can I do?"

I took a step backward, eyeballed her from head to foot, and prayed a little prayer. "Do you have teeth?" I asked. "Yes, honey, over there in the cup. I just don't wear them around at home," she replied in her toothless Southern slang.

Annie Fay was about five feet four inches tall and her husband was six feet six inches tall. She was wearing a pair of her husband's bibs rolled up twelve inches at the ankle. She also was wearing one of her husband's flannel shirts with the sleeves rolled numerous times in order for her hands to stick out. It wasn't exactly a pretty sight to behold. Her blond hair was tied back in a medium-length ponytail with a rag.

In a caring voice, I simply asked Annie if she had any girl clothes.

"Sure," she replied, "I have a closet full of them."

"How about if you bathed, made your hair pretty, put on a pretty lady's outfit and maybe some cologne, and met your husband tonight at the door with a warm 'hello'? Put your teeth in. Your smile is beautiful when you have your teeth in your mouth and not in the cup. I recommend that you try this, and I am pretty sure you will be noticed," I advised. "Show him the lady he married and that you still care for him."

"You think so, honey? I can do that," she offered. So I prayed with her and left.

On Sunday, she came walking up to church with a big smile on her face, looking as pretty as ever, and exclaimed to me, "It worked! Thank you, honey!" God is good. Every time I saw her after that, she looked like a lady and she was a much happier person.

Elsie

Then there was this other lady who was Annie's friend. When she saw that Annie was pleased with my advice, she asked me to come over for a chat. Okay, I began thinking that the life of being a pastor's wife can be a busy one but interesting.

This woman was a three-hundred-fifty- to four-hundred-pound woman named Elsie. She too was a Southerner, but her slang wasn't as pronounced. She stated with a straight, dead serious face, "My son is nine years old now and starting to notice things. Do you think I ought to stop letting him take a bath with me?"

Ted was a pretty good-sized boy, and with her and him in a bathtub together, well, I don't want to envision the scenario. I appeared to cough to get control, catch my breath, and answer her. "Dear God, help me," I prayed silently first. "Elsie," I explained, "you are making the right decision. Yes, you need to stop allowing Ted to bathe with you. You need to teach him the laws of modesty and that men and women need to be separate for private things like bathing and dressing, etc. The private view of a woman from that point on ought to be when he marries the love of his life in the future." She took it well and said she would begin right away stopping the duet in the bathtub. God is good.

Dorothy

Just out of curiosity, how many times do you get this type of calls? Ring! Ring! "Hello, Elaine speaking."

Dorothy is on the other end but is not identifying herself, just simply stating a fact: "It is getting pretty warm out. When is the pastor going to come and take off my storm windows?"

I responded, "Oh, you need your storm windows removed?"

"Of course, I do. Do you think I want to sweat and stay awake all summer from the heat when my windows can be opened?"

After relaying the message, pastor graciously found time in his schedule—which already included working a forty-hour-a-week night shift, sleeping daytime, and tending to church responsibilities—to go over and remove her storm windows.

Then in the fall, a call came in which included no formalities such as "hello . . . this is . . ." Instead of the general introductory information, I just heard: "It is getting cold at nighttime here. When are you going to put the storm windows back up? I can't afford to heat the outdoors, you know."

My long-suffering husband put them up for her. Bless her memory, as she is now with the Lord. Ya gotta love 'em.

Louise

Here is a story about an experience I had but do not recommend duplicating to anyone.

In one of our churches, a lady called me late at night about two hours before my husband had to leave for work. She asked me to come over right away because she had a demon in her house. She wanted me to help her get rid of it. She didn't live too far away and lived with her teenage children. I left our children with my husband who was sleeping. I stopped at a local gas station to tell the proprietor, who was a member of our church, where I was going and what I was supposed to be doing.

Well, I got to the house and was allowed in immediately. The dear lady showed me her house. She had cleaned all day. She had paisley lampshades, paisley couch cover, paisley chair covers, paisley tablecloth, paisley curtains, and lots of other things in her house. There was not a lot of room but a lot of paisley. She told me the problem was upstairs. She had a King Shepherd dog with a huge head. I made good friends with the dog and patted her head very gently.

The lady opened the upstairs door and said, "It's up here." I timidly let the dog go up first, I followed the dog, and the dog's owner was behind me. At the top of the stairs, the dog became agitated, and her hair stood on end. Now that kind of freaked me out, and I began to pray silently.

The lady came up, and she said, "Look, the room is clean, the rug is shook, the bed is made, and their clothing is all put away. I have not been upstairs for about a year. I know my children are clean and neat and take care of their things, but I want you to look here." Immediately behind me was a closet door. She opened the door and what did I behold?

She said, "Here is the demon." I took a good look and smelled a bad whiff of something. I immediately informed her that this was not a demon—it was fresh marijuana. It was hanging wall-to-wall in that room on lines two inches apart from one another with electric heaters on the floor under every third line of plants. Every heater was on, and the room was very warm. The air was very pungent and almost overwhelming.

The lady told me she knew what it was. She said, "My dear children planted them as flowers in little milk cartons early in the spring. They transplanted them into larger milk cartons when they got bigger. Then they were large enough to plant outside. It gave me a whole beautiful hedge around the back perimeter of my yard. Now I always wanted a hedge around my yard. I praised them. I was very happy to see they did that for me and thanked them profusely. They were very careful and watered it every day all summer long. My beautiful hedge was about as tall as I am, very bushy and thick, and made my yard private. I came home from work yesterday, and it was gone. The entire hedge was gone. That was yesterday. Today, I find this."

"Well, what will you do?" I informed her that it wasn't a demon; it was marijuana, and she had better get rid of it quickly.

She said, "I plan to tell their father. He will be here in three weeks to see them."

I proceeded to inform her that this will not be here in three weeks. "This will be on the market in a week, and you will never see it again. Get rid of it now!"

"How can I do that? I don't have any way of disposing this, and I will not call the police on my own children."

Now this was in the Vietnam era of America, and authorities were not very well appreciated, especially in Madison, Wisconsin where we were living at that time.

With a quick silent prayer and a lame thought, I told her I would take it. I told her I had a police friend that would take it from me and dispose of it properly. "He won't know that it's from your house and that I confiscated it from you, and he will get rid of it for me, I'm sure."

"What can I do?" she asked. "How can I do that? How can we do that!" "Well," I offered, "let's stuff it into garbage bags, preferably large lawn and leaf bags." She didn't know it, but I saw her son secretly tiptoe by the stairwell below just then. I began praying lots, "Help me, Lord." I knew I was taking his fortune away. It was worth thousands of dollars.

That is just what we did. I had two or three bags stuffed to the brim. As I dragged them out to my car, I stuffed them into my trunk. I prayed with the dear lady. Then I hopped into my car. Whew! Was that smell ever strong! At that point, the thought hit me: what if I was stopped by a policeman and not the one that I knew personally? I began to pray, and I prayed and prayed and prayed and drove very carefully.

About five miles later, I pulled into my parking lot. I backed into it close to my side door. I unlocked the door and proceeded to drag the bags of half-dried marijuana into my bedroom. When the last bag was pulled in and the door shut, my husband woke up. Now he is a very heavy sleeper, and fire alarms and smoke detectors have never awakened him up to that point. He sat right up straight and literally shouted, "What is that terrible smell?"

"Don't get excited!" I said in a soft voice as the children were sleeping. "It is only marijuana."

"What?" he shouted. "Marijuana? What are you doing with marijuana?"

"Please don't shout," I said in a soft voice. "The children are sleeping. I picked it up at Mrs. L's house. Her boys planted it, watered it, cared for it tenderly, and put it outside for a beautiful hedge for her. Yesterday, it disappeared. Today, it was in her attic hanging on lines and drying for a big sale. It was worth a few thousand dollars, I'm sure." I didn't tell him that her older teenage son saw me stuff it into my car.

"What do you plan to do with this?" quizzed my husband with a little softer voice.

I replied, "Don't get excited. I will call Brother Lou. He will dispose of it for me, and I won't have to tell him where I got it."

"You are crazy!" he said. "You should not have taken that."

"Well, I'm thinking I probably shouldn't have, but now I have it, and I need to get rid of it. It is time for you to get up for work. I will call Brother Lou to see what we can do."

While my husband was dressing for work as a security guard at downtown Madison, I called Brother Lou, the police officer.

"Sorry, sister, I won't take that," he replied. "We cops have to give an account of this and take a whole day off work without pay to appear in court testifying about what we have done. That marijuana is your problem, but you better get rid of it."

Whoops! I really did it this time! I told my husband I had to get rid of it myself. He was in a frenzy. He had to leave for work, and here I was with two little children and three big bags of illegal marijuana. "Whatever will you do with that?" he asked.

"Well, don't worry. We have an incinerator. I'll just take it down there and burn it."

So I dragged one bag down and stuffed it in the incinerator. It took quite a few newspapers to get it started to burn as it wasn't quite that dry, but I did get it to burn.

I kissed my husband goodbye, sent him off to work, and went to the basement with another bag of half-dried marijuana. Just then, the outside door opened and someone came running downstairs. It was my husband, and he was in a panic.

"Do you know what you're doing? It smells like a giant pot party outside! You are going to have every cop in the county here, and they'll find you."

We were in a housing development complex of forty-eight units. I checked outside, and ours was the only one with a chimney that was smoking. My husband had to leave for work, or else he would be late. He figured he would be called home to take the children while I was hauled off to jail. I told him not to worry, that it would be okay, and God would take care of me.

Off to work he went. Me? Down to the basement I went with the last bag of half-dried marijuana. Well, I ended up having to find every old sock in the house that had a hole in the toe to stuff into the incinerator to get that green marijuana to burn. It took a number of trips to the basement to complete the task. When I took the lid off the incinerator downstairs, the odor was unmistakable. The outside air was thick. The last trip I made, I found it getting a little harder—in fact quite hard—to climb the steps back to the apartment. I think the strong smell was getting to me.

It worked. I got rid of all the marijuana. I slept really well that night. Nobody came to the door asking about my incinerator. When I awoke in the morning, I thanked the Lord dearly for protecting me and my family. I am sure to this day that I cannot truthfully say "I didn't inhale."

The Tweets

I must also tell you about the Tweet family. It was at a time in our lives when we managed an apartment complex unit in Madison during the Vietnam era. One early Sunday morning, I received a phone call from Mrs. Tweet. She asked me to please come over. She wanted to see me. I had a little time before I needed to get the children ready and get to church, so I complied and went over to Mrs. Tweet's house.

When I got to her house, she invited me in and immediately asked me if I would like a cup of coffee. Thinking that it probably would help her to talk if I had coffee with her, I ordered the coffee. She served us both coffee and sat down at the table across from me, and I asked her what was on her mind. "Well," she said, "my husband passed away last night."

"Please know I am so sorry to hear that," I replied. "That is terrible. Where is he now?" I asked.

"Oh, he's in the bathroom. He died in the middle of the night, I think. He got up to go to the bathroom and never returned. This morning, I asked my girls to go check on Daddy. They came back and said, 'Mommy, he's leaning over the sink, and he is cold and stiff. He won't talk to us, Mommy. Please come.'"

"Well, did you call the undertaker?" I inquired.

"Yes, they are on their way," she replied.

I immediately thought, *We must get these girls out of the house.* One little girl was six, and one little girl was maybe eight. I called a family from the church to come and get them and see that they got to church. She came right away and took the little girls. I did not want them there to see their dead daddy hauled off.

Little did I know what a good call that was. Soon after the little girls left, two hippie-looking gentlemen, walking a Beetle Bailey walk, came in with a zippered body bag. "Where's the body?" they asked. "It's back in the bathroom," said Mrs. Tweet. They found the way themselves.

I tried to make small talk at that point as I could hear bones breaking, some clunking around, and a zipper bag being closed. In no time at all, I saw the two men walking out, one with the body slumped over his shoulder like a bag of beans. The other one opened the door for him.

It just so happens that my husband was coming over to check on me about that time. He saw this weird hippie van, all painted up, sitting outside Mrs. Tweet's apartment. One man opened the back door to the van, and the other one flopped the body bag off his shoulder with a big heave onto the floor of the van. *Ker plunk*. Needless to say, my husband was a little shocked at what he saw, but nothing was unusual in Madison during those years.

At the funeral home during visitation, the little girls were playing hide-and-seek and making faces in the mirror on the wall behind their daddy's coffin. The lady seemed okay with it, and the girls did not seem at all upset. So much for that experience.

Sandra

Oh yes, there is a story about Sandra I must tell you. Sandra loved the Lord. She was a believer in the Lord Jesus as her Savior. She was a single mom as her estranged ex-husband was a drunk. She was trying to make a living for herself, and God blessed her greatly. One day, she confided in me saying, "Please help me." She had determined to stay single and care for her family and be a good example for them. At this time in her life, she was being severely tempted. It seems there was this man she would run into periodically in the course of a typical day. There wasn't much way to avoid him. However, she seemed very attracted to him. She found herself driving by his establishment often just to see him. She didn't stop her car; she just drove out of her way to see him more often. It was like he was a magnet. "What can I do?" she asked. "I do not want an involvement. I plan to stay single. This man is a married drunk. Why do I feel this way? Help me please."

"Well, Sandra," I replied, "last week, you told me you were taking ginseng everyday and feeling really good. I think you better get off the ginseng you have been taking. It is an aphrodisiac amongst other things, and you don't need that. If you stay on that, you may end up in trouble."

She asked, "What is an aphrodisiac?"

"Well, as far as I know," I replied, "it can be a sex enhancer. I have read about ginseng. Yes, ginseng might help you feel better, but you don't have to feel that good. You had better stop taking it. I think it will help you to get off of it."

The next time I saw Sandra, she told me she went off the ginseng. She was feeling much better and totally embarrassed about looking at that man in a romantic way. She was glad he never knew the way she was looking at him as she was always in the car driving by. End of that story. God is good.

Lily

Lily was a sweet little lady in the church. During the years we served the church, Lily became a widow. One year, we had a huge snowstorm/blizzard. Everyone had to clean their roof from all the heavy snow piling up. Pastor tried to help her, but little Lily, who was between seventy and eighty years old, was on the roof shoveling her own snow. She did not want to risk the liability of someone else getting hurt on her property.

When she came down from the roof, she began to put on snow skis. "What are you doing?" I asked.

She informed me that she skied out to her mailbox and back every day to get her mail. She also skied around the perimeter of her property. She had a trapline baited and set. She checked the line every day, emptying and throwing away all the mice that she caught. She said that she kept the mice out of her buildings and out of her house that way. She said that for about six months, there hadn't been any mice in her traps, so she must have caught the ones that were close to her buildings. Lily was very matter-of-fact; she told how things were, and that's how they were, no embellishments. Lily was a strong, hardworking lady, but most of all, a dear Christian sister who is now with the Lord.

Bertha

Bertha was an older single lady; I think she was widowed. Bertha lived in a fairly nice home in the forest but all by herself. Bertha didn't mind having company. She loved the pastor and his family, especially his boys. She loved to cook a huge meal, feed our family, and send us home with all the leftovers. She always said, "I don't want any leftovers at my house." On one of our visits, she shared an interesting story.

She would sleep on the sofa which was right in front of the big picture window. Her porch was on the other side of the window. She was awakened one night by something walking across her porch, stomping, and making a lot of noise. She looked out the window and saw a bear taller than her. She was sure it was the neighbor man trying to tease her and wearing a costume of a bear to get a rise out of her.

She put on her housecoat and opened her door wide and screamed, "You might think you're funny, but you're not funny, so you can just go back home."

To her surprise, it wasn't the neighbor man. It was a real bear, and he grunted back at her, just as loud as she was yelling. Bertha stepped back into the house and grabbed a horn that her late husband had left for her. It was her bear horn, she said. It was to frighten away the bears (and she showed it to us). She blew the horn loudly that night, and the bear ran away. Her comment to us was that she would rather have a bear at her house any day than a strange man.

When we first moved to that church, Bertha invited me over for a ladies' meeting. While I hadn't even heard the church had ladies' meetings, I told her that I would be happy to come. When I got there, twelve ladies were there, and I didn't know any of them other than Bertha. It seems that was the community meeting. The group handled a little business, had a big snack, and then Bertha took the floor and announced that we have a guest with us today. "Elaine is going to speak to us. She has moved in and will be a part of us." Well, now . . . that was the first that I heard about this. I didn't know anyone there, I didn't have anything planned to speak about, and I didn't know what they were expecting me to say. My husband used to say that he learned in Bible college that a pastor must be ready at any moment to speak, to pray, or to die. Well, today, that fit the pastor's wife.

I whispered a little prayer and decided to start at the beginning and give the testimony of my faith in becoming a Christian believer in the Lord. I explained that Jesus died for my sin just like he did for their sins. From the moment I believed that, I have been a Christian in learning more and more how to love my Jesus. I am so thankful someone told me about this. I know for sure when I die, I will be in heaven because God promises, "For whosoever shall call upon the name of the Lord shall be saved." The Bible says also, "I go to prepare a place for you, and if I go to prepare a place for you, that I will come again and receive you unto myself."

I told the ladies that I was happy to be at their meeting, happy to be in their community, and living in the forest. I told them I liked it there and enjoyed all the beautiful wild birds and the wild animals we could see nearly every day all around us. I told them that I felt, indeed, God was very good to me to bring me there.

The meeting was over, and I was asked if I could take one of the little ladies home. Everyone there was over thirty years older than me. While in the car, the little lady I took home asked me if I was really sure that I could really know I was going to heaven when I died.

I had a wonderful opportunity to share many scriptures with that little lady and show her that she too could become a believer and a Christian. She did that that very day. She prayed the sinner's prayer asking the Lord Jesus to save her and make her a Christian. Soon after, that little lady developed cancer and died. I am looking forward to having a visit with her in glory someday. Thank you, Lord.

Christie

Christie was a dear friend from Minneapolis. She called me one day and asked if I would please take her on visitation to witness for the Lord. She wanted experience and training in how to witness about Jesus.

So we went together to visit the lady on the lake who had just lost her husband. She was grieving, and I felt she really needed to hear about the Lord Jesus. We sat at her kitchen table where she was smoking and drinking a beer. She told us all about her husband and was happy to have someone to talk to. After a bit of talk, I asked her if I could share a little about the Lord Jesus with her. She coughed a little and said, "No." She said she had a bunch of things to do first. She must first take care of her husband's affairs.

She said, "You see my husband was a Mason. They had a service for him, and he is in heaven today because they took care of all of that. They will take care of that for me too because I am a Mason."

"Well, can I tell you how you could know for sure that you are going to heaven by the Bible way?" I asked.

She replied nervously, "No, I trust in the Masons, and they are very good to me. They will do fine."

She talked longer and every effort we made to turn to Christianity was put down with her refrain: "My hope is in the Masons."

Then she moved on to another beer and another cigarette for her to enjoy. We prayed with her, and for her, and then we left.

The next day, I heard she had a stroke. She was unable to speak a single word. She was moved to a nursing home and did not live very long. We never saw her again. I thank God I had the opportunity to tell her about Jesus. God only knows if she ever trusted him. I called Christie and told her. She was very touched and moved and grateful for our visit. What is so remarkable for her was we were both so thankful that God led us to her that day. God is good.

Chapter 3

Home Life

There were lots of times in our family life in the ministry when we could feel and know the hand of God upon us.

We had just moved to a new ministry location, and my husband was diligently seeking a job. He finally was hired as an orderly in a nursing home. Most of our ministry years, it was necessary for my pastor husband to work a secular job to support the family as the churches we served were rather small and financially unable to adequately support a pastor and family. I had two small children, was expecting the third one, and at that time unable to work. Times were rough financially, but we were making it, knowing God was going to provide.

One Sunday morning after I had everyone dressed for church and had cleaned up after preparing breakfast, I looked to see what to cook for dinner. To my dismay, we had no potatoes, no meat, no bread, no butter, virtually nothing to cook. I told my husband the bad news. I did not know how to feed our family that day. Pastor said, "It isn't your job. God will take care of us. Let's just pray about it." So he prayed that God would give us our daily bread.

We went to church that day on that prayer. When we returned home, we were greeted by a piping hot casserole, a loaf of homemade bread, a pound of butter, and a dessert sitting on our doorstep! Is God good or what? We had a feast of that meal. To this day, we never found out where it came from. The only person we told of our need was God. Isn't that just like a good God? He is so perfect and good to us! The next day was payday, so we could then shop for our needs.

There was another time in those lean years when we were all in the car waiting while pastor was making a visit to the hospital. The boys and I were waiting in the car when one of them stuck his foot up in the air and said "look." I looked, and I saw a new hole in his tennis shoe. "Well, boys, we'd better pray for money to buy new shoes for you boys." Right there in the car, we prayed that our dear Lord would give us money to buy new shoes for our boys.

All the boys were getting tired of waiting in the car and asked if they could go play on the field at the edge of the parking lot. I told them they could play in the grass if they stayed out of the parking area and away from the cars. They got out of the car and started romping around in the grass, running and tumbling. It wasn't long before Tim came running up shouting, "Mama, Mama, look, God is going to give me new shoes. I found some money."

In his hand was a wrinkled, wet, faded $20 bill. Sure enough, God showed our boys how he can take care of his own. It was a wonderful lesson they still remember. I think we were able to buy more than one pair of shoes that day. Thank you, Lord.

One day while living in the forest community, I forgot to close the garage door. It was Saturday night, and we had house guests. I was awakened very early from a noise in the detached garage. I looked out the window and saw a bear in the garbage in the garage. I put on my housecoat and stepped out on the front porch. I told the bear to get out of my garbage and get up the hill where he belonged. The bear looked at me, grunted, and ran up the hill. He obeyed me! In the meantime, my husband woke up and saw the event. When I got back in bed, my husband was chuckling and stated that my curlers scared the bear away. Well, maybe. Anyway, it left.

On another occasion, I had stopped my car on the way to church because a big bear was sitting in the middle of the narrow road. I watched him a while, then rolled my window down, and shouted, "Get off the road. I need to get to church." He moved, and I arrived at church on time.

Wildlife was plentiful in that community, and one morning while driving our boys to school, we saw a spectacular event. Two horses were running madly around the upper fence line of a paddock. They look very angry, were very loud, and their ears were laid way back on their heads. We stopped along the road to see what was happening. There was another horse in the center of the field rising up and pounding the ground over and over again. Soon he joined those running at the edge of the field, and the horse in front went to the same spot in the middle and began pounding the ground.

At that point, we left the scene to continue our journey to school but wondered what we had observed happening. On the way home that night, we asked the farmer who owned the horses. We explained what we saw, and he told us the horses had killed a timber wolf. He said they were wild until he came up to water them around noon. He saw that they had been pounding on a wolf until it was as flat as a pancake, including the skull.

We loved the night music of the animals. One evening arriving home in the dark, we thought we would hear the whip-poor-wills. It did not happen that night. We turned off the car, opened the door, and heard a ferocious roaring growl coming from the garden. We turned the lights toward the noise and saw a giant papa bear standing on its hind legs yelling at us. He seemed quite angry that we caught him in the garden. We cautiously ran one by one to the porch and into the house leaving the bear to do his pleasure. The next morning, we found that the bear had dug up a half row of potatoes. He left them laying there unharmed. He did not eat them—maybe we scared him off too soon or maybe he liked them cooked better.

It was a few years there when I remembered that while in Madison, I prayed for a nicer place to rear our family. This country living was a gift from God in answer to my prayer. The boys loved it. They would hunt squirrels and rabbits, sneak up on wildlife, and learned so much about life in the woods. I will never regret that opportunity. God is so good.

There was a day when my husband was home, and the boys and I were away. My husband answered a phone call in which a man wanted a ride to the doctors' office which was ten miles away. "I will be right there. What's up?" inquired my husband. The man answered, "Stay home. I'll be right there." He arrived very soon and stepped out of his car holding a red farmer's handkerchief in his hand. He calmly said, "I just cut my finger off. Can you take me to the doctor to see if he will sew it back on?" Then he unfolded the handkerchief showing the severed finger to my husband. Pastor took him to the doctor's, and they fixed his finger.

In all of our ministries, we included our children. They were in the ministry as much as we were. When we had a crisis or someone we loved had a crisis, as a family we would pray for that particular person or that particular problem together. When that problem was resolved, together we thanked the Lord for answering prayers.

Each of them trusted the Lord Jesus fairly early in life, and it was very exciting watching them grow in their faith.

Every evening at bedtime, I would go to their rooms and quiz them a little on the meaning of creation, rapture, etc. Then I would ask for their private prayer requests for the day. I would pray for them then. Next day at bedtime, we shared answers to prayers first then new requests. It was a beautiful time alone with each of them. I continued that practice until each of them left the home as adults.

Pastor Smith always encouraged the church to try to read the Bible through in a year. That inspired us to purchase cassette tapes for each of our boys that they might be able to read the Bible through in a year as well. So for Christmas, we bought each of them a cassette player, and they began playing a portion of a tape each night following along in their Bibles. They, indeed, did read the Bible through in a year and also learned how to pronounce all the big words by following along with the tapes as they read. It was a thrilling experience for us as parents to see these boys growing in the knowledge of the Word.

Because our churches were small, our children did not have a lot of peers to play with at church. Our second son complained to me that he did not want to be the only one in his Sunday school class. I suggested that we pray for a little boy his age to come to Sunday school, and that's what we did.

Well, the very next week, a new family came to church, and they had a little boy just my son's age.

After about three weeks of getting to know this family, our little seven-year-old invited his new friend to go to the basement for a man-to-man talk. A deacon was in the little side room downstairs, counting the money from the offering, and heard them talking. He told us Tim was leading his new friend to the Lord Jesus. He shared the whole plan of salvation with him just like he remembered his daddy told him about.

Another time in his early teen years, our eldest would catch fish, clean them, and deliver them to senior citizens in the area who could no longer fish for themselves but loved fresh fish. He was good at it, enjoyed it, and was blessed as were we and the seniors as well. He, of course, was loved by all that knew him for his kindness.

Our youngest consistently insists that he trusted Jesus as his Savior when he was just three years old. He said he was under the coffee table, and we were all talking and having fun, but he was praying for salvation during that time. He giggled when he told me and said, "I didn't tell anybody. It was a secret until today." It was months later when he told me about it. Amen. Thank you, Lord. He is now pastoring a little church in Northern Wisconsin.

I was told that I would be living in a glasshouse if I were to be in a parsonage or a manse. Oh well, my kids had flaws, and I was made aware of them time and again. I decided early on that I only had to answer to God for my boys' behavior, so I listened to the complaints and simply responded, "Okay."

Other times, I was told that a man used my house during church to discipline his son as my door was unlocked, and he expected screaming.

The best story is when my cupboards were raided because someone needed flour or sugar or an egg for the potluck meal, so they helped themselves. When I discovered that, I began making sure all my doors were locked during church.

I considered motherhood a special privilege. It was my prayer that my three children all grow up secure, knowing they were loved, knowing about the Lord Jesus, and desiring to follow my God as a Christian. God honored that. They all became believers at young ages. Pastor and I decided early on to homeschool our children. It was not very popular back then, but we felt it important to train them ourselves. We ordered a curriculum which cost a thousand dollars a year, and we did all the work ourselves. I loved every moment of homeschooling. We had so much fun being creative, taking hikes, chopping wood and stacking it, physical education class, you know it. I will never regret the time we spent homeschooling and training our own children. It wasn't very popular back then, almost unheard of by many. It was not easy but very rewarding, and I would do it again in a flash. We had community Christian friends who took our boys for weekly trainings for various skills. They worked with them, teaching them skills for life. They learned carpentry, small motor repair, electric appliance repair, and other essential skills.

Pastor Smith was called by the public school principal one day and accused of having his children being truant. He proceeded to explain that his children have not missed a day of school, have not been tardy, do their homework, have tests, and are doing quite well in school. The principal became very irate and cursed at my husband. My husband hung up the phone, not willing to listen to that kind of talk. In a few moments, the school superintendent called and apologized for his principal and his behavior. He asked for a visit from my husband.

My husband packed up the attendance charts, the testing grades, report cards, the curriculum, and the textbooks and went to talk to the school superintendent. The superintendent said, "Mr. Smith, it takes us months to develop a curriculum. We have a lot of people involved and work hard at planning on what we should teach. How do you know what to teach?"

My husband explained to him that we purchased a ready-made curriculum, proceeded to take it out of the envelope, and show it to him. He was very impressed and possibly quite shocked. He had never heard of homeschooling before and didn't know there was such a thing. He leaned back in his chair and asked my husband a question: "What would it take for me to have your children enroll in my school?"

My husband answered saying that was a fair question. "I'm not against that," he told the man. "If you promise me three things, I would seriously consider putting my children in your school."

"What?" inquired the principal with much curiosity. "Go ahead and ask."

So pastor said, "Number one, can you promise me no teacher will ever swear at my child?"

"No," said the superintendent sadly.

"Number two, can you promise me that my children will not be offered tobacco, drugs, or alcohol on campus?"

"No, I am afraid I cannot do that," said the superintendent sadly.

"Well, can you promise that my children will not be bullied on the bus?"

The superintendent sadly hung his head and said, "We cannot do that, either. I understand, Reverend Smith. Will you then please call the state education department and register your school?"

The conversation was finished, they shook hands, and pastor left. God is so good.

Are There Really Angels?

On a balmy Wednesday evening in early spring, we were enjoying a lovely prayer meeting in the north woods of Wisconsin. After the service, a huge storm developed. I was driving my car full of people, including my three boys, three other boys, and a little grandma. We were on a major highway where logging trucks often traveled. I could not see the road as it was raining so hard. I saw a little reflector and told the grandma that I was going to turn there because it might be our road home. She thought it was probably a sign in a shallow ditch.

I took the chance because I didn't want to be run over by a big logging truck who couldn't see me on the highway in time to slow down. I could not drive very fast as visibility was terrible. I figured truckers were up higher and could see enough to go faster. I prayed a quick prayer, and at about five miles an hour, I made the turn. Thank you, Lord, it was the road! We traveled at that speed a couple of blocks distance when a big deer walked out in front of us and stopped between the headlights of our vehicle. It stood there and winked at us. The whole carload saw it wink and stand there still. I, of course, had to stop the car and wait for him. During that time, a huge wind with tremendous power rocked our car and passed over the area. Then it was still; the rain stopped, and the deer walked away. We were free to go. Some of the kids said they were scared; others said, "I am praying!"

The next day while passing that area again, we saw that a huge tree, half the width of the car, had been uprooted and was swept across the street from where we were stopped. It was about ten feet from where we would have been.

If it had not been for the deer, we would have been struck by that huge tree.

Granny said, "I think we had us an angel!" I think we did. Thank you, Lord, again.

God Works in Unusual Ways

Not all of us can have a very unique opportunity that God entrusted us with such as reaching a Chinese Buddhist for the Lord, but we all can relate to home missions. In the very essence of the Word, Deuteronomy 6:6–7 says, "And these words which I command you to this day should be in thine heart, and thou shalt teach them diligently to thy children, and shalt talk of them when thou sittest in thine house, and when thou walkest by the way, and when thou liest down, and when thou risest up."

The Bible does not specify what ages of children to teach. My children are all adults, but I still am obligated to follow his commands. 1Timothy 4:12 says, "Be thou an example of the believers."

A number of years ago, a little Chinese girl who was enrolled at our local college came to our church asking to see Pastor Smith. She was told that the Baptist church would help her if anybody could. She told pastor she needed a safe place to live. He sent her to me. We made an appointment with her, and that Tuesday, she was there promptly, and I interviewed her. This is her story.

"I am an only child of two parents who love me very much. I have been trained to study hard, play the piano, and be a good girl. My parents have sacrificed very much to send me to America that I can study hard and learn well. I am so shamed in America. In my dorm, there are boys all around even on the bunk over me. They . . . they have no shame. I moved to an apartment on the third floor with a Hmong girl, and she started having boys over. I had to move to the living room floor, and I am so ashamed. They don't even have all of their clothes on." She began crying. "I need a place to live where I can study, be safe, learn well, and be a good girl," she pleaded.

Who can say no to that? I tested her out. I said teasingly, "If you are Chinese, you will drink tea with me."

"Oh, yes!" she said. We had tea. Then I said, "You must come play my piano." She was very happy, sat down at my piano, and played "Yankee Doodle" beautifully. I promised to try to help her, prayed with her, and she left.

At that time, our family consisted of me, my husband, and our two adult sons, so we had a family powwow. We decided it would be fun having this girl move into our home for a year. The boys would love having a little sister. She wanted to live with brothers.

We invited her over, and she met the boys and asked them if they would be her big brothers. That struck the macho button in them. They puffed up, stood tall, smiled, and said "sure." Then, she wanted to shake hands on it. "This is what Americans do," she said, "to agree." They shook hands on it.

Moving day came, and we got her all settled in. I fixed up her room to look feminine and even found a Chinese painting for her wall. She asked me to treat her like a daughter just as if she were mine and asked if she could call us Mom and Dad. From that time on, she was ours. She won our hearts.

The first night, I explained all the noises in the neighborhood. I explained about the curfew whistle noises and the ambulance and police car sounds which were all within three blocks of our home. She was grateful for the explanation, for she had heard all those noises before and didn't understand what they were. She had been frightened by the mysterious sounds. I asked if I could pray with her before she went to sleep. She answered, "I will like that." I prayed that God would keep her safe, to bless our new daughter, and give her a good night's sleep. She was thrilled and thanked me profusely for the prayer.

One house rule that we had was that we were Christians, and everyone living here must be in church every Sunday. She replied, "I would love that!" She never missed a Sunday.

Although her name was DuLi, she asked me to give her an American name. So I asked her what her name meant. She said it means a pretty flower like an orchid. Upon that comment, I suggested that she take the name Orchid, and she did. She still goes by that name, and I think she enjoys it.

Orchid usually cooked her own food, but she ate with us at the table and learned to wait for us to say grace before we ate. She always whispered softly, "Yes, yes," during our prayer. She seemed to enjoy each time we prayed. She enjoyed attending church services every Sunday morning.

Orchid was a very adamant student, spending hours until late into the night studying hard at every class assignment she had.

Every class for her had to be translated into her home language for understanding. It took a great deal of work. She would ask us many word meanings, and often, I would get the trusty dictionary out, look it up with her, and explain it, so she could remember it longer than if I just told her the meaning.

On Orchid's first night in our home, while studying at the dining room table, Scott, our son, came tiptoeing behind her and pulled her beautiful Chinese braid. Just like a typical sister, she turned and belted him in the stomach with her elbow. Then she tattled on him, saying, "Mom, Scott pulled my hair." She always wanted that in her life, she explained. She and Scott became instant friends. We knew she was a good match for our home and a keeper.

It wasn't very long into the semester when we discovered she was talking on the phone to a gentleman in Iowa. She told us he was a friend from China. She had known him as a classmate in high school. He was a little older and a student at a university in Iowa. He was getting his master's in international marketing statistics.

We told Orchid to invite him to Thanksgiving dinner at our home in northern Wisconsin.

She was excited. He said, "No, you have a good thing going. I don't want to wreck it for you. I have been in America four years and have not been in a home."

I took the phone from Orchid and said, "Cloud, this is Orchid's mom. I want to invite you to a traditional American Thanksgiving dinner at our home. Please come."

"Yes, I will!" said Cloud (for that is his name).

"Come and stay a few days," I offered.

"Yes, I will love that," said Cloud. "I will see you at Thanksgiving time."

One day after that, Cloud was talking to Orchid on the phone and asked if we could have a Bible study with them while he was here. She asked pastor if they could have a Bible study. Of course, we were more than willing, and we did have a six-hour Bible study across the table with Cloud, Orchid, the pastor, and me. What a beautiful time we had! Pastor started the study with creation. Cloud understood that. He said it made more sense than evolution ever did. Orchid could not understand sin. She was a Buddhist and always tried to do good. Pastor explained the Ten Commandments, and she understood. "Yes, I have sinned," she admitted. What a blessed time together.

We were so glad that Cloud joined us for the Thanksgiving holiday. Our family loved him, and we had a great time. We made a lifetime friendship. Cloud returned to Iowa as his school is there. Cloud and Orchid continued their friendship via telephone.

One day about three weeks later, Orchid hung up the phone, turned to us, and humbly said, "Mom, Dad, Cloud and I, on the phone together, just prayed that Jesus would save us and make us to be Christians, too."

Praise the Lord! What a wonderful, wonderful proclamation to hear. "Thank you, Lord. You are wonderful!"

We are still in touch with Cloud and Orchid, and they still love the Lord Jesus. Amen.

Chapter 4

Me—A Secretary?

One year, I was in the business world. I loved the job, but I am not a secretary. That year, I was a secretary. It was a spring day, and I wanted to be outside. The boss came in saying, "I have a client one hour away. He does not believe in banks, so you need to go collect $10,000 cash from him for me." Hallelujah! I get to go outside.

I was driving on this lonely road in my little Ford Festiva, praising the Lord, and asking for an opportunity to witness for him. The boss was a sweet believer and would appreciate that. Just then, around the corner were two young Native American men carrying all their worldly possessions on their back. I waved and zoomed by. Just then, it hit me: there is my witness. I abruptly stopped, rolled down my window a little bit, and backed up. When I got to the men, I hollered out the window, "If I give you a ride, you won't rob me, will you?" (Is that stupid or what?)

"No, ma'am. We're trying to get to California. The bridge collapsed, and we want to see if our families are alive. We're going to Duluth, Minnesota, to catch a plane to California and would appreciate a ride."

In my heart, I knew this was who I was to witness to. I opened the doors and invited them in.

"You must be an angel of God to give us a ride. Thank you!" said one of the men.

I said, "No, but I work for him. I have a message for you from him."

"We prayed to the great spirit for a ride. I'm so glad you stopped," said the other man.

"I am here today to tell you the great spirit has a name. For this ride, I want to tell you about the Lord Jesus Christ, the creator of the universe.

"Hey! Turn the radio off," said the man in the backseat. "I want to hear this too."

"You men must be hurting since it is the middle of the workday, and you are carrying your worldly possessions while walking down the street. I believe I can show you a better way of life."

"You got that right. We just left an AA meeting and have no job, no home, and no money. Our families are in California and may have been on the bridge that collapsed. We can't reach them by phone, so we're trying to get there quickly. We are very worried."

"Well, the Lord Jesus loves you today and wants you to have a good life. Jesus Christ is the God of the universe, the great Creator, and the salvation of our soul. God did not make us to flounder in life. He did not make us to be alcoholics, to be homeless, to be jobless, to be lost in this big world. God loves you and wants you to have a secure life. You can know God in a real way. He is a loving father who has a much better life for you than you have ever known. He wants you to know the Lord Jesus, his son, who can give you the power in your life to become productive, happy, and secure. Jesus Christ is the one who died on the cross to cover your sin and forgive you. The Bible says whosoever shall call upon the Lord shall be saved. Jesus wants to save you from a wretched life. He will forgive you and set you on the right path."

"Wow, that is heavy! I know I am a sinner," said the man in the backseat.

"Me too," said the other one.

I reached my turn off point then and pulled over to let them out to finish their journey.

I did not lead them to a decision. I urged them to think about what I said, gave them each a very clear Gospel tract, and encouraged them to find a church when they got home and to be sure the pastor believes and preaches the Bible. I encouraged them to pray to the Lord Jesus asking for forgiveness and his help but to know it is a serious thing, and God is for real.

"A good man who believes and knows the Bible," I said, "will show you more about this Jesus whom you really need to know. Will you do that?" I said a prayer for them. Then I left them there. God only knows if they followed up. His Word is powerful; I trust him.

I finished my trip, picked up the money I needed to in cash, and headed back to the office. I sang all the way back. It was a great day at the office, I figured. I didn't have to sit at a desk. God blessed me, and two men heard the Gospel plan.

Another time, I was a teacher with four paraprofessionals under me in a four-county area. I was to train the others on how to teach parenting skills to parents of preschoolers needing help in learning.

That all went okay, but I had a personal challenge. My students were school-age and needed lots of help. They were brother and sister and lived with their mom and dad. There was a lot they had not experienced, and my job was to broaden their horizons. One assignment I gave to their parents was to walk with them four blocks down the street on the sidewalk, looking and naming everything they saw. Examples might be a squirrel nest in the tree, a doll shop with toys in the window, a dog tied up to a porch, etc. They were to walk every day naming everything they could see and check on the assignment paper if they did it. When I returned in a week, I looked at the paper, and I saw that the work was all done; they did it every day. I praised them for their willingness to help their children. I asked them how the children liked it. "Oh, we didn't take the children, just the two of us went, and we loved it." So back to the drawing board, I asked them to do it again taking the children with them. After another week, I checked, and they had done it, and the children were amazed at all the things in their neighborhood. It was the beginning of the world for that family. They were so much fun! What a personal joy and challenge! I loved it.

Chapter 5

Chaplaincy Service

For over twenty-four years, pastor and I have had the precious privilege of being chaplains with our local police force and county sheriff's department. We volunteer with the two departments, the officers, and in the community when needed. Our services have been needed in many critical situations, such as the Ladysmith flood, the devastating Ladysmith tornado, debriefing clerks from bank robberies, families in crisis, major debriefings, drownings, fires, car crashes, and assisting the officers with death notifications. God has been gracious in allowing the county to provide us with specialized training. We have been all over the country in various training sessions, so we can provide quality care to those in need. That valuable training has also served us well in our own ministry.

A few years into the chaplaincy program, Dave and I decided to get credit for all the training hours we had spent.

At that time, we enrolled in the master program at the International Conference of Police Chaplains, or ICPC. I did a thesis on "Turnkeys and Headsets," better known as jailors and dispatchers. I passed the training and completed the paperwork. I then received my master's degree in chaplaincy.

One of my favorite parts of the chaplaincy has been to visit the inmates in jail. At this time, I would like to share some of those stories I experienced over the years. I hope they are encouraging for you to read as they are for me to remember. Of course, as in other segments of my story, all names have been changed. Believe me though, there are no innocent ones.

Since pastor and I lived right in town, we carried the pager for notification. It was usually evening or nighttime when the jail had need of a chaplain, so I answered the call.

This particular nighttime, around ten thirty or so, I was paged out by the dispatcher who said there was a very distraught lady who asked for a chaplain to come talk to her.

There is a little conference room in the jail, so I had them bring her to me, and we were locked in that room for a visit.

Here was an approximately sixty-year-old lady just fidgeting with her fingers and crying, "Help me please. Can you?"

"What can I do for you this evening?" I inquired.

So she began her story. "I am a society woman. I am from Minneapolis. I am wealthy and donate to lots of charities. I made a wrong turn, ended up in the ditch in a snow bank, and the police came. Yes, I had been drinking, but I am not drunk. They brought me here and made me put on this nasty orange clothing. I broke a fingernail, and they will not give me a file. (Can you imagine that?) The judge is gone for the weekend, and it is Friday night. They said I am here until Monday after business hours when I can get a judge to hear me. I must shower and live with the common criminals in that cell down there, and I am scared to death. I am so humiliated."

I replied, "Those ladies down there are just like you. They have been caught drunk driving, bouncing checks, etc., and they are not any danger to you. You all are watched and checked on frequently. Trust me. There is no danger for you here. However, as a chaplain, I have a question for you."

"What do you know about the Lord Jesus Christ?" I asked. It was like magic to see her response.

Almost like a reflex, she gasped a deep breath, lowered her head, and wept. After a moment, she looked up at me and began talking. "I gave my heart to the Lord many years ago and promised him I would live for him. Wow! Have I ever forgotten that! Dear God, forgive me," she prayed. "I have wronged you."

She then looked at me and said, "Thank you for asking that question. I am here for that reason. I will never be here again. I have not been in church for a long time. That will change. May dear God forgive me. I will again dedicate my life to him, and I will change. I will be the person I should have been all this time. I will never go to the casino again nor will I ever drink alcohol again. I shared a scripture verse with her, prayed, and left her in a much better mood than when I found her. She thanked me profoundly, and I left rejoicing. I never did see her again. I pray she did change. God is good.

One of the most dreadful things that a jailer does not want to experience is a suicide in the jail. Well, one night around eleven o'clock, I received a call from dispatch. It seems there was a very distraught inmate who needed help and needed it now. They asked me if I would please talk to him to see if I could please help. They did not know what to do.

I was in bed, so I got dressed and went down to the jail, praying on the way that God would help me like he always does. They said the man was in the holding cell. I saw him. He was wearing orange, curled up in a fetal position in a corner, shaking, hyperventilating, and crying.

I asked him if we could talk. I asked the jailer if he was safe for me to talk to in the conference room. They assured me he was safe. So the two of us were locked inside the conference room for a visit. He was able to walk but still had all the symptoms as before.

I whispered a quick prayer that God would help me know just what to say. I asked him if I could read the Bible. He nodded yes. I turn to Psalms 139 and began with that beautiful chapter about where we can run from God; he is always there and always knows us. As I read it, he sat up a little straighter in his chair. Then I turned to John 3:16 and read, "For God so loved the world that he gave his only begotten son, that whosoever believes in him should not perish but have everlasting life." He quit crying. I turned to John 14 and read that chapter. His breathing quieted down. I turned to Genesis chapter 1 and read the entire chapter.

Then the man sat up and spoke. "Well, I am a good person," he said.

"I am sure you are," I spoke confidently. "Most people I know are basically good people, but you have made bad choices in your life. You have toyed around with the devil, immorality, and drugs."

"How do you know that?" he asked me.

"Well," I answered, "you have demonic and lewd tattoos all over your arms. And you don't end up in jail for going to Sunday school too much.

"Well, the tattoos on your arm tell a lot," I answered him. "I believe you have made some very bad choices in life. Bad choices can destroy a wonderful life. A life is not meant to be as miserable as you have been."

"Yes, I have been miserable. I have a voice in my head telling me to kill myself . . . kill myself . . . kill myself. I cannot sleep at night. I see terrible visions when I close my eyes, and I hear that voice over and over."

"That is the devil trying to destroy you. We can get rid of those thoughts and those words in your head tonight if you are willing."

"I am all ears. Please help me. I will do whatever you say. I want free from this anguish. Please show me how I can get help."

At that point, I had him read Romans 3:23 out of the Bible. Then I had him read Romans 6:23 out of the Bible. Then I had him read Romans 10:13 in the Bible.

We talked a little about what those verses meant. I asked him if he understood them. I told him that I was a sinner and that God had forgiven me. I asked him if he thought he was a sinner. "Yes, I know I am," he responded.

"As an unforgiven sinner, God does not have to answer your prayers. God is a loving God. He cares for you like a beautiful father would care for his son. He wants to help you, forgive you, cleanse your heart, and make you free tonight. God wants you to forsake your sin life, turn from it, and ask him to forgive you and make you free. If you can be sorry enough for your sin and ask the holy God to forgive you, he will send your sin as far away as the east is from west. My wonderful God will become your Savior and forgive you and make you free tonight if you will that."

This man fell upon his knees and began praying the most humble prayer that I have ever heard. He confessed many sins and asked if God would please forgive him. He then asked if God would please save him and heal him. He also asked if God would take away all that evil, all the voices in his head, and thoughts in his mind that are wrong.

When he finished, I prayed a little prayer as well. Then I asked him if he had any relatives that had been praying for him. He said, "Yes, my grandma. She is a sweet lady." I told him Grandma's prayers were answered today. I also asked him if he knew any children's Bible songs that he remembered from a child. He thought for a moment and said, "Yes, I do. I remember Zacchaeus. My grandma used to sing it to me."

"Well, when you go to bed tonight, hum that tune, and God will give you the sweet peaceful sleep that you have not had in a long time."

We got off our knees, and I wish everyone could have seen his smile. It was radiant. He was a new man in Christ.

I called for the jailer. He came and took the man back to the cell. The inmate was walking tall and humming and looking good.

Because he was a high risk, I always go to the dispatch center and give a report. When the jailer returned after locking him back up, there were five people in the dispatch center other than me. The jailer asked, "What did you do to him? He is totally different. He is changed!" Amen!

I love it when the jailers asked me those questions. I held up my Bible and said, "It is the power of God to change a life. Can I show you more?" They always say no, but thank you anyhow. The jailer then proceeded to tell everyone that the man was standing straight, smiling, and humming a tune. He was amazed. Is God good?

Shelley

I simply must also tell you about this lovely lady whom God changed. I have been so blessed with the privilege of teaching the Set FREE! program to the ladies in jail. It is a beautiful program dealing with all kinds of addictions and packed full of scripture.

Well, this lady Shelley had a bad addiction problem. She asked if she could join my class. "Of course," I answered. I never refuse anyone who is sincere.

I knew she was not a believer, but most of them are not when they begin the class. Almost everyone trusts Jesus as their Savior by about the third lesson.

We began, and there were three or four ladies in the class. There were about twenty-five or more Bible verses in each lesson. Each lesson usually took more than one session. I began by showing them around in their new Bible that I gave to each one of them. I showed them Genesis, Psalms, Matthew, and Revelation. I explained the difference between the Old and the New Testaments.

Shelley was eating it up; she loved these classes. At the end of each lesson, there was a whole page of homework each student must do to stay in the class. She was very faithful in attendance and in doing homework.

I think it was about the third lesson when I had to be gone for a weekend. Shelley was in her cell studying her lesson when all of a sudden, her sin life hit her square in the face. She started chanting, "I need Jesus! I need Jesus!" She would not quit. The jailers came and asked her if she wanted a chaplain. "Yes, I do," she answered. So two lady chaplains came to help her. Shelley was beside herself chanting over and over, "I need Jesus! I need Jesus!" The two ladies then prayed to Satan to leave her alone. Shelley freaked out. She lost it; I believe she had a breakdown. At that point, she saw demons coming from every direction trying to attack her. She started screaming, "Get them out of here! Get them out of here!" So they asked the chaplains to leave the area.

At that point, Shelley was scaring her inmates. They wanted her out of there. So they put Shelley in a safe cell all alone. They sent the two chaplains home and watched Shelley closely for any danger she may cause herself.

Shelley took her Bible with her to the new cell. She didn't talk to anyone after that. When I got there on Monday, I asked to see her. "No, you don't want to do that." I was informed. "She had a mental breakdown and won't talk to anyone," said the officer in charge.

Well, at that point, all of the officers were new. I had been there a number of years, and I believe they trusted me when I said I want to talk to Shelley anyway. "I want to see for myself." So they let me talk to Shelley. The liaison officer stood, pretending to fix a hinge just next door to where I was. I know he was listening. There is a little trapdoor at just about knee level in her cell. It is for passing her a food tray. I lifted the flap and called for Shelley.

Shelley came running to the door, stooped down, and said, "Oh Elaine, I am so glad that you came. Thank you." The officer next door was surprised that she talked to me and coherently at that. Shelley told me, still holding the Bible with two hands, that she needed Jesus.

"Shelley," I said, "you need to make Jesus Lord of your life." Just then, Shelley crossed her eyes, her head down, and in a very guttural voice said, "I can't do that." At that point, I knew I was fighting for her soul. I prayed a quick prayer for wisdom. Then I said, "Shelley, you need to make Jesus Lord of your life." Again Shelley lowered her head, spoke very gutturally, and said with her eyes cross, "I can't do that."

At that point, I instructed Shelley to repeat after me. I said, "Say, Jesus Christ is my . . ." She said, "Jesus Christ is my . . ." Then I said, "Lord." Her voice turned guttural. She crossed her eyes and said, "I can't do that." At that point, I shouted "Lord. Say it!" She said, "Lord."

Shelley was a new creature. The oppression was gone. She was smiling and thanked me. "Oh thank you, thank you. What a relief. I am free. Jesus is my Lord. Jesus is my Lord."

Her whole countenance was changed, and she was praising God, thanking him for hearing and helping her.

The officer next door heard it all but stayed silent. He had to have been touched.

I gave her a couple of scripture verses to read in her Bible. I prayed with her and left her. Shelley was from another county, and we were housing her because we had more room in our jail. Because she needed special care, they sent her back.

After three weeks, Shelley was still on my mind. I asked our liaison officer if I could go to her county and visit her at that jail. He checked with the county, and they invited me over.

I put on my beautiful golden seven-point star badge, took the chaplain squad car, and drove over to her county. When I arrived and told their officers whom I wanted to see, they laughed and said she won't talk. She only holds and reads the Bible, showers with one hand holding her Bible outside the shower, and changes hands and switches sides. She says she is fasting and won't talk to anyone.

"That's okay, I want to see her anyhow. She's my friend," I said.

"Okay, your choice." And they let me in to see her.

She came running up to me and said. "Elaine, I am so glad you came."

The officers were shocked. She actually talked to me.

We sat down, and I said, "Shelley, what happened to you?"

So Shelley proceeded to tell me her story.

"I was back in Ladysmith studying my twelve-step class. It was on the Ten Commandments. Just then, it hit me; it overwhelmed me. The more I thought about it, the more I knew I had broken every one of them. I dishonored my parents, I took God's name in vain, I cheated, I lied, I stole, I even murdered. I had an abortion and killed my own baby. It was more than I can handle. Those two women chaplains freaked me out, and I had to get them out of there. Thank you so much for showing me Jesus. I am set free, and I know it. I want to learn all I can, and I read my Bible all the time."

I shared a couple of scripture verses with her, prayed with her, and left.

It seems she found a safe home in Northern Michigan that was very structured to help her with her addiction. She was allowed to move there and wrote to me every month. After six months, she moved to a southern state to reunite with her family. She was writing to me monthly, always thanking me for showing her Jesus. She got a good job as a manager of the convenience store in her hometown. Her children loved her again, and her parents were all reunited as a family. She wrote to me and thanked me again and again for showing her the wonderful gift of salvation. God had changed her, and it was for real.

The letters quit coming after a year or so. After a couple of months, I called to see how she was. Her mother answered,

"Shelley passed away from an aneurysm six weeks ago. Her veins were very weak from her drug history, and she could not recover. If you are the one that helped her get her life back together, thank you. We had our Shelley with us again."

I know I will see Shelley in heaven someday. God is so good all the time.

On another occasion as a chaplain on call, I was asked to speak to a new believer, a twenty-one-year-old man, awaiting possible sentencing of up to fifty years in prison. He was guilty of transporting men from Minneapolis to Wisconsin for the purpose of stealing guns. He knew just where they could find some and would take them there. The deal went bad. The owner came home, and they tied him to a tree and shot him dead. He became an accomplice to a murder.

His dad lived in a homeless shelter—a long-term alcoholic. His mother had married a man that wanted nothing to do with him. She also was an alcoholic. He had a girlfriend who just delivered his baby. He so dreamed of giving his child a warm loving home like he never had. He had been in so many foster homes and detention centers where he was always sent home and told to go straight. That wasn't meant to be.

He had a home full of crime, became a great liar, thief, and crook, and knew well how to live on the street. He had nothing to offer a child as the government saw it. The child would be adopted, and he wasn't even allowed to prove his paternity.

His girlfriend was incarcerated for theft. He had no job, no friends, no home, no education, and no money. His only asset is that he has a wonderful Savior, and he is thankful for that. He was recently saved in the jail with another chaplain talking with him.

He needed a listening ear that night. He admitted he was guilty of everything he was accused of and deserved his sentence. He is upset because he needs to pray and read his Bible and have some quiet time with the Lord. Every time he tries, he is bombarded with profanity, lewdness, and filthy language coming from his cellmates. That is jail life.

He needed a little encouragement and a listening ear. I shared a few verses with him and prayed with him. He thanked me, said I helped him, and he knew he could make it now. He was a new Christian since being incarcerated.

I asked if the officers had a place they could move him in for the night, and they did that. God blessed him.

They were gracious, and again, God is good.

Again, one evening, I was called to the jail as a man there was suicidal and on a suicidal watch. He wanted to talk to a chaplain. He was determined to "do himself in" and had tried a number of times previously.

I simply showed him the difference between heaven and hell and asked him which one he was ready for. I assured him that one of those places was his eternal destiny. Then I asked if I could show him the way of salvation. He agreed.

After having him read many verses of salvation out of my Bible, he told me he knew he was a sinner and would like to know a loving God. He repented and asked a holy God to change him and make him a new man in Christ. He asked God to forgive all of his many sins and help him never to do them again. He asked God if he could only be dependent upon God from now on. He asked God to save him and give him peace.

I prayed after he did, and he arose from his knees as a new man in Christ. We chatted a little, I gave him a Bible and told him where to start reading, then called for the officer to take him back. He said he would read that Bible, sing Christian songs to himself, and begin attending every Bible study and chapel service the jail had to offer from then on.

Again the officer was stunned. The man was changed. God does that. Isn't God good?

On another occasion, we were called out in the middle of the night for a death notification. Sometimes officers, and even hospitals and medical professionals, need help from chaplains in some situations. This was one of those situations.

Two teenagers were speeding and playing games on the road with a friend. The driver tried to pass the car and lost control of his vehicle. He and his buddy were both ejected from their car. The driver died. The passenger was airlifted with probable neck injuries. It was my job to go to the police station and notify his friend that his buddy did not make it.

He was pretty much under the influence, but he was pretty upset as well. He took it very badly. I had taught him in school a few years before that. He used to heckle God. He also taught other kids how to drink. Tonight he was extremely sobered. This boy asked me that night if I would pray for him. I did pray for him, and I asked God to help him change his life and learn to trust God.

It was not a pretty sight seeing him this upset. It was also not a pretty sight at the hospital with his friend dead. It is never easy telling someone their friend or loved one has died. Without the grace of God, I don't know how anybody handles it. God is gracious, and I'm so glad we have such a wonderful God we can count on.

The chaplaincy program is very diversified, and in our county, all of us are volunteers. One very hot summer day, we were called to assist a driver along the highway. An officer was there and needed some help. Arriving at the scene, we found a man quite disoriented sitting in his car in the hot sunlight. He told the officers he was sitting there because there were a bunch of pachyderms crossing the street in front of him. His car would not run, and he had sat in that hot car for too long.

The officer asked me to coax him into my car. It was the chaplain vehicle, but it was not marked as a squad car. He would not get in a police car. It was my job to get him out of the heat into my air-conditioned vehicle and get his driver's license from him. The officer was unable to do that as the driver did not trust a policeman. He was afraid they would arrest him, and he did nothing wrong. We needed to find out who he was and where he was from. I was asked to get the name of a relative from him. He did not like talking to a policeman, but he would talk to us.

I asked him for his address, and he could not remember. At that point, I said, "Show me your license, so I can call home and get some help. Surely, your family will come and help you."

He didn't comply, but the officers were able to get enough information to contact his relatives. It seems he was lost, took a wrong turn, and was about fifty miles from where he should have been. His car was out of gas. I convinced him to come to the chaplain office at the courthouse. I told him it would be cool there, and he could wait for his family to come and get him. We did that. It took over an hour for them to come. We talked about pachyderms and how he liked them. Needless to say, there were no pachyderms in the road that day, but I never argued with him, and we got along famously until his family arrived.

That is one of our more entertaining chaplain calls. I enjoyed that experience greatly.

Too many of our calls were death notifications. Pastor and I would often go together to assist the officers with that job.

One time while making a notification at the hospital, we had to divide two different families into two groups, separating them to two ends of the hospital. They were fighting over whose fault it was that the man died. We had to calm each group down and offer comfort and keep them away from each other. The hospital staff was upset and was complaining to us because of so many people in the ER. We offered to send them home if the doctor chose to do so. He said, "Please get them out of here."

We asked each group if there was a home they could meet in as the hospital was too busy for this many people to hang around. They complied and soon left. The hospital staff thanked the chaplains, and we went home.

On Labor Day of 2002, our little town was hit by a big tornado. Our entire church building was destroyed, as well as most of the city. The basement of our church and the freestanding bell next to the building were left.

While Pastor Smith groped his way through the rubble, trying to find the general area where our church building used to be, I stood for hours at the front door of the courthouse. Individuals and groups came by the dozens. Many of them had chain saws, others were medics, others for search and rescue, and my job was to direct each group to the direction where their job was to be assigned. There was a workstation for each volunteer type.

For the next two weeks at home, I was on the phone literally from morning until bedtime. The phone would not stop ringing. People all over the country wanted to hear our story. Radio stations and TV stations were often interviewing my husband at the site, and I was answering telephone calls with people asking, "What do you need? How can I help out?" It was a tear-jerking, humbling time for us. So many people, groups, churches, organizations, other states, and even a couple of other countries called to see if they could help. God was so good to us to help us through that extremely busy time.

Our church received gifts or money every week after that for many months to follow. Every Sunday night, pastor would read the mail telling of the gifts others had sent to bless us. We worshiped and praised the Lord together for his goodness.

Chapter 6

Amazing Testimonies from Overseas

We have, over the years, been extremely blessed traveling to various countries and hearing testimonies of believers from around the world. At this time, I would like to share some of these beautiful testimonies of God's choice servants. All of their names are changed or used with permission to protect the security of their ministries. I am most humbled to have been able to meet them and listen to their amazing stories. All of these stories are true and as accurate as my memory allows. Some of the stories were told to me in English but not all. Each one of these stories was told to me, personally knowing that I was writing down each story to share with others.

In Mexico, we were thrilled with the wonderful way the believers worshiped the Lord through singing. They put their whole heart into it. It was beautiful, and I will never forget it.

In England, we were surprised at how quiet and private the folks were. Everything was proper and orderly and quiet.

The folks were believers but typically British and proper and quiet.

Scotland was a different story. They robustly sang praises to the Lord. Every service we attended while in Scotland included the beautiful hymn "Amazing Grace" to the tune of "Londonderry Aire" (Danny Boy). We loved it. They would always sing all the verses even if there were six of them.

In Ireland, again they sang robustly as they did everything else there. It was the most like the United States of those countries we visited. We visited homes and witnessed to folks.

In Ukraine, the people were very warm and very sincere in their faith, seeming so appreciative of the opportunities they have, even after the communist wall came down.

One sweet, sincere lady invited us to visit her classroom in the public school in her village. We did, and she was teaching the Biblical story of Abraham and the substitutionary sacrifice God planned for Abraham's son Isaac as found in Genesis 22. She told her students she hoped to see them in heaven one day and how to get there. She then dismissed the class as school was over.

Each student there had a job, like clean the board, sweep the floor, clean the bathrooms, the corridors, etc. Everyone stays an hour after classes each day to clean the building and grounds. A great idea. Think of the money they save not needing to hire people to do this. Also, the students learn to take care of things better, knowing they may have to clean up after themselves.

Then this dear had tea for us. She offered cookies and tea while we listened to a concert of some of her students on the bandura, the national instrument of Ukraine. It was beautiful, like an inflated guitar.

Then the teacher looked me in the eye and most sincerely thanked me, on behalf of all the United States believers, for praying for them during all their years of oppression when Christianity was not allowed freely in their country.

Then she shocked me into reality by saying matter-of-factly, "Now we are praying for your country to once again have this freedom we enjoy." Wow!

The churches we visited in Russia were very friendly, but fear still lurked in their hearts. They were spied on for so long in their every move, they still had mistrust in talking too much to anyone about their faith. They were very discreet about it for fear it may be taken away again. It may be, at that. It was a good experience to witness these feelings. I pray we never get to that point in the United States.

Mookabot

This is the story of a Central Asian lady who was formerly a Muslim but now a Christian. Her name is Mookabot. She was living in Turkey at the time I met her. Mookabot related this story to me during one of my visits there. Although spoken in the Russian language, her dear friend translated to me in English. She told me to use her name, so I will tell the story as much as possible in the first person.

> I lived very poorly in a poor village. We had a house where the bricks were crumbling, and the windows rattled. We had animals but no barns or shelters for our animals.
>
> I was very oppressed and very sick. My husband could not find a job, and we had nothing. I was possessed by a demon and could hear voices in my head all of the time. I could not eat, and I could not sleep well at all. I was getting worse all the time.
>
> I went to visit my mother to ask her what I should do. She told me to go with her to see the mullah. A mullah is a Muslim priest.
>
> Together we went to visit the mullah. He did some antics over me and then prayed over me to Allah. Then we went home. My life became worse. I went to the mullah again. I was desperate for help. The mullah did pretty much the same as before. After the third visit to him for the same problem, he sent me home.

He said I was doomed. He said I must be one of those people who are possessed, and I must learn to live with it.

Later while sharing the verdict with my mother, she came up with a new idea. My mother told me that when she was a little girl, she heard about a God in Russia. She said that the God of Russia was a God of love and forgiveness. She didn't know his name nor anyone else who knew his name. She said he was very powerful, though.

I began that day to pray to the "God of Russia." I prayed that he would find me and reveal himself to me. I prayed that he would love me, heal me, and give me a baby boy.

He did that for me. I had a baby boy. I knew this was a wonderful God, and I thanked him. I still did not know his name nor anything about him.

While caring for my young son, things became very difficult for me with my depression and those awful voices in my head telling me daily to kill myself. It was getting more difficult to eat or sleep, and I was becoming very ill.

About that time, my sister called me from Turkey. She asked me if she could send me a ticket to Turkey. She would get me a job there. I may start to feel better, and I could send money home to my husband. He would fix the wall and windows and maybe even build me a kitchen and also a barn for the animals.

My husband was happy about this possibility. He would stay home with our children who were all in school by now. I was to send him my checks.

While in Turkey just a short while, I met with my sister, and she had news for me. She told me she was a Christian. She said her God could heal me, save me, make me well, and that he loved me very much. She said he is the God of Russia, and his name is Jesus Christ. He is the great Creator of the world, and he loves you and me.

I immediately fell on my knees and thanked God for revealing himself to me. I confessed all of my sins and begged this loving God named Jesus Christ to forgive me, to save me, and to heal me.

God did just that! Immediately, the voices—those terrible voices and feelings in my heart and head were gone. They left me. I had instant peace in my heart that I never knew possible. It is still there today; God is so wonderful, and I love him.

Neither my sister nor I knew much about this God or about Christianity at all. However, my sister said she knew Christians ought to be baptized. So we secretly met in the night at the river, and we baptized each other. We want to do everything we can to please this loving God. He is wonderful, and I pray to him many hours a day telling him that I love him.

I want to spend more time praying to the real God than I did to Allah.

My son and daughter-in-law had met her five months previously. The day after meeting her, they had to leave for America. She told them her story that day. She did not know any Bible verses or had ever seen a Bible. They gave her a New Testament to keep. It was in her language, but the Old Testament had not been translated yet. She was totally thrilled. As she hugged her own Bible, she said, "My very own copy of God's Word to me." Mookabot thanked them over and over and was just delighted.

Five months after that time, my family returned to Turkey. They found her and invited her over for a service. She was delighted to meet a Christian and then see a house full of them. They worshiped together and sang hymns.

Mookabot said that she had been reading her Bible every opportunity she had. She said that she had read through it many times, and she wanted to learn what it was all about. She also said that she did not understand it and needed help.

I arrived in Turkey about that time, and I met her. She told me her story and asked me to teach her about the Bible. My daughter-in-law is a trained translator and was very willing to help us out. What a privilege it was to explain the Word of God to someone who knew nothing at all about it.

I was there for three Saturdays, and she came each of those days and had me explain the Bible to her. I had the wonderful privilege of telling her all about creation, salvation, and Christian baptism. I also was able to answer many of her questions. She would read the Bible and save her questions for me on the weekend. She was just radiant for the Lord!

She told me her son and daughters are saved. She fasts from four until seven o'clock daily that her husband would be saved and come to know her Savior. She will return to her homeland in April, whether or not all of the repair work on her home is finished. She knows they have new bricks and windows so far. She will work now for money toward a kitchen and an animal shelter or barn.

While she is fasting, she is asking God for her husband to know the Lord. She is asking God for the proper time for her to tell him she is a Christian. If she told him about it while she was in Turkey, he would not let her come. He is a Muslim.

When she tells him of her new belief in Christ, he can do one of four things:

- He could say he truly loves her and become a believer too.
- He could beat her terribly. She said she wouldn't mind that because he's done that often anyhow. She could put up with that.
- He could divorce her. She doesn't want that as she loves him.
- Her husband could legally take her out to the desert and abandon her without food or water and leave her there. That is all legal in her homeland.

As far as we know, Mookabot's husband is still not saved. She is now in another country working and sending money home to him. She is a great witness for the Lord to all the ladies she meets wherever she goes. Pray for Mookabot when you think of her. She has a hard life but is very happy in the Lord.

I am so blessed and feel so rich for having had the opportunity to meet her and share the precious Word of God with her. She is a dear friend I will never forget. I think of her often and pray for her often.

A Man's Testimony as Told to Me by Him

I am thirty-two years old. I lived in East Asia which was part of the Union of Soviet Socialist Republics most of my life. I have two elder brothers, three younger brothers, and one sister. We were poor; my grandparents lived in one room of our small house. They had no pension and no money. We all lived together in the Soviet Union with no competition, no name brands, and everybody was like everyone else. It was under communism, and God was not acknowledged.

I, however, was a Muslim. Every day, I would lock the door and privately worship Allah. I had to keep it secret as worship to a god was forbidden.

When my papa died, my grandpa grieved terribly for two years—crying all day, every day. Then he died. But there was no God for comfort. When one died in the USSR, the country allowed a funeral with a mullah. The mullah had the family memorize a chant to comfort the family and help the dead go to the other world. Believe me, it was no comfort.

Schooling stopped at age eleven in the Soviet Union system. Then there were private schools for the exceptional students. At age twelve, I moved to another village to attend prep school and to live at the school. At about age fourteen, questions were in my mind about who I am and what God is.

I asked one of my teachers who God was. "Oh, there is no God. We are communists," he said. Another teacher had me memorize a prayer to Allah and repeat it five times a day. This teacher taught evolution and that I came from a monkey. None of these teachings made sense to me, and I was not satisfied and kept looking.

At the school, we had to learn the *Numoz*. It was deeper Muslim training. All boys in the exceptional school had to have this training. After testing, nine of us boys were chosen for special training. We were told we would have a nice career, make big money, and become a mullah. We learned and passed a pharmacy test. Then we were sent to Turkey for further training. I did not get to see my mama for a long time. I heard that my brother was addicted to opium but wasn't allowed to go home and help him.

I was given huge books to read, no pictures, and very difficult to understand. After reading a big book, I was given another big book with different things than the other book said. I was very confused. Each book contradicted the previous book. The mullah teachers still practiced other things. They were not nice people.

I was in the teacher's room one day and saw a whole bunch of porn videos, lots of them. I reported him to a teacher higher up and was reprimanded and punished for doing so.

At age eighteen, I drank to rebel and used opium. I lived in a hostile way, worked, smoked, drank, and caroused all I wanted. I had problems at home. My brother stole my mom's ring to buy opium. My sister died. At that time, I was on opium and was hallucinating from it. I was on the run, hiding from authorities not to be found, so I could go to my sister's funeral. The embassy could not find me.

Finally, a friend saw me and made me call my mama. The friend gave me money to go home. It was good to see my mama again. While there, I lived on marijuana and parties all the time. It was a bad life. So at age twenty-five, I decided to change my life. I went to Antalya to live. I returned to the Numoz to be clean.

I could not find peace studying about Allah. I knew there had to be a creator. The books about Islam did not agree even with each other nor mention the creator. I was really confused. The material I read was so corrupt, and Mohammed was so vile in his life. I was so confused that I called on genies, demons as you know them, to enter my life and help me. What a hopeless situation it was in. After a few days, the demons entered. It was the scariest days of my life. I became a very angry person, saw a lot of evil everywhere, and fought against evil and the demons. I wanted to be free from them; I hated them.

They said if I can find someone to forgive me, they would leave me and let me go. I said bad words, had evil eyes, and had powers so no one could touch me. No one wanted to be around me. They tied me up with ropes, beat me, and then called the ambulance. I saw the medical personnel and could see their sins and blotted them out. They all beat me again and again at the hospital. My eyes were abnormal, my blood pressure was okay, and they found no physical problems, so they let me go.

I lost my job, nobody wanted to be around me, and I was miserable. For two years, I searched the Quran and found no answers. Someone told me that if I read the Torah, I could understand the Quran better. I looked everywhere but could not find a Torah. I looked online on the Internet. There, someone offered me not just the Torah but the whole Bible—Old and New Testament—for free.

Also, a man on the Internet offered to answer any of my questions about the Bible. I read the Torah to see if it would help me understand the Quran. It was so interesting to read the Torah that I read the New Testament as well and finished the whole Bible in eight months.

I was told of a home church meeting and attended it. I was angry there because they were praising God for allowing them to gather, and they gave testimonies of God. I left, but the next week, I returned. I prayed that I might learn the truth as I was so confused. A friend saw me reading the Bible on my break at work and offered to explain it to me. He was kind and explained the entire Bible, Genesis to Revelation, to me. That's it! I understood and left the room. In a private room, I fell on my knees and thanked God for opening my eyes to the truth. I trusted Jesus as my Savior and became a Christian. I have learned what real love is and am now learning about a Christian life and how to please the real God of heaven.

Amen! What a story. Thank you, Lord, that I could witness this transformation. What a great God we serve and how thrilling to have heard these personal real-life testimonies firsthand.

Robert's Story

Robert told me his story while I was in Turkey visiting. This story was told to me through a translator who is very reputable. These people are amazing.

> I come from an unbelieving family of Muslims in East Asia. We attended an orthodox church and were not strong Muslims. At times of funerals and weddings, we thought about God. I was bad, really bad. I stole, beat people up, cheated, and drank. I was afraid of my papa. I knew there was a god, but I feared my papa. He was the one who punished me. When he punished me, I prayed to my grandfather (god in heaven) for help to survive my father's punishments.

I went to Moscow to study. After returning to East Asia, I was invited to a man's house to watch a video. The man was Silas, and it was the only video in the country that was in their own language. It was the *Jesus* movie. Many people were there, and I cried during the movie. I returned three times, crying each time I saw the movie. Then I prayed for salvation to the God of love, and he saved me. I was baptized, then encouraged to study and prepare myself for the Christian ministry to my people.

> Soon persecution began. My family turned against me, and the KGB had threatened my family to leave me. Gas was turned off in our homes, and believers lost their jobs if found out. There were checkpoints so that believers could not travel from village to village sharing their faith.

> Soon after, I met my beautiful wife, and we had a Christian wedding. Then the persecution began again. They arrested me, beat me, put needles under my fingernails, and beat my kidney areas, so they would quit working, and I would die. They tried to force me to deny Jesus, but I would not.

He sent his wife back to her dad to protect her as he was being beaten daily. Finally, a Christian brother said to come live with him that he and his wife may be together.

> I got a job, had a baby girl, and I got a tiny apartment. Our material possessions were two pillows, one blanket, and a carpet. Soon I found another job, so we could buy food.

The believers scattered for fear, and it is hard work to meet for church. The groups are small but faithful, and God blessed.

Another sweet saint talks to me.

A beautiful Christian, former Muslim, lady told me her story. She told me life is hard for the Muslim woman. She is a slave to her husband and to her in-laws. The youngest son must live with his mother. The mother-in-law owns all the babies, teaches them, cuddles them, bathes them, and dresses them. The mama can only hold her baby while she's nursing. The mother-in-law takes full charge of the children. If the mama objects, the mother-in-law will have her son beat his wife. If the mama doesn't obey the mother-in-law or the husband immediately, she will be beaten. They work hard in the garden, do all the laundry by hand, and do all the cooking, cleaning, and shopping. They have no break, no recreation, and no peace. It is a miserable way to live and no hope for any other kind of life. There is no love in a Muslim home—only anger.

This lady and her husband became Christians. The first thing her husband said he had to do was to tell his wife that he loved her. The next was to start showing it to her. She was shocked at first and thought he was going to dump her for a new wife. A lot has changed in their home life, but she still has no say in the lives of the children. We American women have no idea how fortunate we are.

There are a number of fascinating stories I would like to repeat of believers in controversial lands, but I do not want to hurt my fellow sisters and brothers in the faith.

I know we should never stop praying for these dear believers who have been beaten, electrically shocked, drugged, imprisoned, and had foreign things rammed under their fingernails trying to get them to deny Jesus Christ, their Savior. They need daily strength and our prayers.

One man invited us to sit at his table as he told us his story. For Christianity, he was imprisoned for around sixteen years. His family was allowed visiting privileges once a year, but it was all the way across Russia to Siberia in order to see him. They went as often as possible, spent a few short days, and returned. Many years, they had a new baby to introduce to him. His church was wonderful and helped the family survive all of those years of hardship. His family members were adults when he talked to us. He was released because his wife and our own President Reagan, at the time, complained to Gorbachev to release the religious prisoners. He denied having any but checked it out when they gave names and addresses to him. He released them, including this dear brother, and gave him an apology check amounting to enough money for him to go home and buy land, build a house, and live comfortably. His skills were adequate in all parts of building as he learned all he needed working as a prisoner in Siberia. He taught his boys to help, and it was a beautiful home. His boys are now all serving the Lord faithfully, pastoring Christian churches unashamedly. What a hero of the faith.

He was so miserable and about to die from fasting in prison, having been told his family would never come again. They told him that his family was told he was dead and that they would never write nor visit again. The food was terrible, and his living conditions were worse. He was told if he wrote his name on a paper denying Jesus the Savior, he could be free. Each year, they offered him that. He refused, knowing God would take care of him. He did. God is always faithful.

These are tremendous testimonies of God's saints. It makes me ashamed how little I do for him.

Conclusion

These recollections make me think of a pen of lambs I saw one day. Walking up to the house, I passed their pen, and they immediately jumped into the fence thinking I was going to feed them. It seems the farmer had to hand- or bottle-feed this group of lambs. Every person they saw was expected to bring food. I pushed them out of the fence they were stuck in, and they jumped right back and became stuck. They just don't learn very quickly.

It is no mistake that Jesus is our Shepherd, and we are the sheep. Sometimes we are slow to learn what we need to know and do what we ought to do.

This has been fun, reminiscing the years I have had serving my Savior. I have seen my parents, and every one of my siblings and their spouses and their children trust the Lord. God is so good to me. It is my prayer that you too will personally experience great joy, knowing and serving our wonderful Lord. That is my story.

To God be the Glory!